Wind in the Sails:
Developing and Maintaining Fervency in Preaching

Wind in the Sails:
Developing and Maintaining
Fervency in Preaching

Dr. David A. Oliver

ASHLEY
BAPTIST CHURCH

2nd Edition: 2024

ISBN: 978-1-387-42063-6

Ashley Baptist Church
10463 Belding Rd.
Belding, MI 48651

www.ashleybaptist.org

Contents

Forward

Wind in the Sails was originally written to help train college-age young men who go out as summer evangelists for Neighborhood Bible Time. It is the perfect book for those young preachers, as it sets forth five different formulas for preaching the truth with a passion that persuades.

When I first read this book, I so appreciated it that I secured several copies to give to my staff, lay-preachers, and preacher boys in our church. I also distributed some at a few of the Christian colleges where I spoke.

My wife Kathy saw the book on my desk, read it, and gave it high marks. She commented that "every young man studying for the ministry needs to read Dr. Oliver's book."

Whether you are a novice or a seasoned preacher, you will find this book profitable. I am so glad to be able to recommend *Wind in the Sails*, and I will continue to promote and distribute it to preachers of all ages.

Dr. Douglas R. Jackson,
Sr. Pastor, Community Baptist Church, Saginaw,
Michigan
President, Michigan Association of Christian Schools.

Preface

Twenty-five years ago, I was invited to speak at the Mid-America Conference on Preaching hosted by Detroit Baptist Theological Seminary. It was my privilege to preach in a plenary session as well as teach two workshops on the subject of preaching. One of the workshops I taught was entitled, "Developing and Maintaining Fervency in Preaching."

Later that same year I traveled to Boulder, Colorado, for a week to assist in the training of summer evangelists for Neighborhood Bible Time. NBT trains college-aged men and sends them to local churches throughout America and several foreign countries to conduct week-long evangelistic meetings for children and teens. I, myself, traveled as a Bible Time evangelist for two summers in the 1980s. Charles B. Homsher, the founder and director of NBT, asked me to come during a week of training to help the young men in the area of preaching. I would teach them and listen to them preach, critiquing their delivery. I thought the session I taught at DBTS might be helpful, and so I delivered it to the summer team. Brother Homsher asked me to return and bring the same material the following year.

The leadership mantle of NBT passed from Charles Homsher to Larry Koontz several years ago, and the location of NBT training has moved more than once. However, after all this time, I continue to assist in the evangelist's training for one week each summer. For a quarter century I have brought the session on fervency in preaching with only slight variation from its original content.

I am very thankful that my small contribution to this ministry has been a blessing to many. Men who traveled NBT years ago have told me that they remember the session on fervency, and that its principles still help them to "come out of their shells" and preach more effectively.

This small book is this workshop on fervency in print form. It is not a comprehensive textbook about fervency in the pulpit. It is a single, concise presentation. My hope is that by putting it in print, it might help men who have heard this instruction better remember it and thus apply its teaching more profitably to their ministry. I also hope that by publishing this presentation, some who are not affiliated with NBT can profit by this instruction.

I dedicate this small book to all the men who over the decades have traveled for NBT, and I dedicate it to the two fine directors the Lord provided for this ministry. To Charles Homsher, who never imagined that his greatest impact would be mentoring men for ministry even more than reaching young people with the gospel. And to Larry Koontz, who so capably fills shoes few thought could be filled. The Lord has blessed their efforts. Today hundreds of former NBT evangelists are preaching the gospel around the globe, serving as pastors, missionaries, evangelists, seminary professors, and Bible college presidents.

My prayer is that God will use this small book to help young preachers develop and maintain fervency in preaching.

Introduction

David Martyn Lloyd-Jones records the following incident in his book *Preaching and Preachers*:

> I was staying in a village in a certain part of England and went to the local church just across the road from where I was staying. I found that the preacher was preaching that evening on the prophet Jeremiah. He told us that he was starting a series of sermons on the prophet. So, he was starting with that great text where Jeremiah said he could not refrain any longer but that the Word of God was like a fire in his bones. That was the text he took. What happened? I left the service feeling that I had witnessed something quite extraordinary, for the one big thing that was entirely missing in that service was fire. The good man was talking about fire as if he were sitting on an iceberg. He was actually dealing with the theme of fire in a detached and cold manner; he was a living denial of the very thing that he was saying, or perhaps I should say a dead denial. It was a good sermon from the standpoint of construction and preparation... but the one thing that was absent was fire. There was no zeal, no enthusiasm, no apparent concern for us as members of the congregation. His whole attitude seemed to be detached and academic and formal.

Everyone who has attended church with any regularity has at some time heard messages that did not maintain the attention of the congregation. If a preacher is honest he must also admit that, yes, he has preached such sermons. While I wish it were not true, I know that I have.

How can a preacher expect a
congregation to listen to him with
rapt attention when he doesn't
seem to care much about the message
he himself is delivering?

It is too easy to blame the congregation for its lack of attentiveness. Unfortunately for the preacher, honesty demands that we admit that an indifferent congregation is not always the problem. In fact, such a crowd can often be made to pay attention by a preacher who knows his business. If the sermon that failed to keep attention was orthodox - if it faithfully communicated God's truth as revealed in the Bible - the problem was not that the sermon had uninteresting subject matter. The truth of God is always "profitable" (II Tim. 3:16) and important. Let's be honest. The problem with sermons that fail to keep a congregation's attention is often an uninteresting preacher. William Quayle, in *The Pastor Preacher* wrote with a touch of overstatement, "The sin of being uninteresting is in a preacher an exceedingly mortal sin. It hath no forgiveness." How can a preacher hope to be persuasive when his presentation is listless and apathetic? How can a preacher expect a congregation to listen to him with rapt attention when he doesn't seem to care much about the message he himself is delivering?

There may be several reasons for a sermon to fail to control the thoughts of a drowsing congregation. I am convinced that one of the primary reasons is lack of fervency on the part of the preacher.

2

Webster defines the word fervor as "intense feeling; ardor; zeal; earnestness; passion." Fervent is defined as "having or showing great warmth of feeling." All Bible preaching should have this characteristic.

Among fundamentalists and evangelicals in the last several decades there has been a renewed emphasis on accuracy of exegesis in the pulpit. This emphasis is a good thing. Paul admonished Timothy to "preach the word" (II Tim. 4:1), not his own personal opinions or biases. Intellectually weak sermons constructed more from imagination than the careful study of the meaning of the inspired text are unworthy of the Christian pulpit.

However, in expository preaching there is a serious danger. Beware of allowing sermon preparation and delivery to become an academic exercise devoid of the passion that is vital in all good preaching! Warren Wiersbe argued, "The pastor who expounds the Scriptures or who explains a text finds it necessary to be specific - but this does not mean he has to be dull!"

G. Campbell Morgan suggested that the three essentials of a sermon are: truth, clarity, and passion. As contemporary preaching ceases to be shallow and sensational, it should not cease to be inspirational. It must be fervent.

Dr. Monroe Parker used to tell his ministerial students a humorous account of an old backwoods southern preacher who was asked by a younger preacher how he "got his preaching up."

"Well," he replied, "first I reads my text. Then I 'splanify it. Then I puts my rousements on!"

This fanciful old preacher may not have been well educated, but he did accurately summarize three important steps in sermon preparation and delivery. Many preachers today are excellent at the first two, reading and "splanifying." Their treatment of the text is exact. Their outlines would earn high grades in any seminary homiletics class. Unfortunately, they neglect to put their "rousements on." Preaching that communicates that the preacher himself is not aroused by the message he is preaching often fails to arouse any interest or response in the congregation.

Several years ago, I paid a visit to my daughter who was then enrolled at a Christian college. Before I took my little girl out to lunch, I accompanied her to chapel. I enjoyed the enthusiastic singing of the student body and looked forward to hearing the preacher for the day who happened to be a member of the Bible faculty. From the perspective of content, the sermon he brought was precise and insightful. He carefully and correctly explained the Scripture passage he had chosen for his text. No doubt, his outline was crafted so as to be a model for his ministerial students to admire and emulate. He even made some helpful applications for college-aged young people. But as I listened, I looked about the auditorium and saw students dozing or looking at their cell phones. Some appeared to be reading notes, perhaps for an upcoming class. Shame on those students, right? Well, not really. I have to confess that the chapel message had not gone on very long before my own mind began to wander. At one point, I actually began to drop off to sleep. I was not a hostile or indifferent listener. I intended to give my undivided attention to the chapel message that day. But I struggled to pay attention. It was hard for me to get anything out of the sermon. Why? This dear man of God failed to put his rousements on! His entire presentation was monotone and lethargic. Although he spoke for only thirty minutes, it seemed as if this preacher droned on for hours. His apparent lack of enthusiasm for his own sermon was positively contagious! It was difficult to resist being infected by it.

It is a serious mistake to believe that content alone apart from delivery is important in preaching. Right doctrine is essential. But right doctrine needs to be delivered in an effective manner - with fervency.

According to Warren Wiersbe, one of the traditions of Welsh preaching that made it so effective in previous generations was "catching the hwyl." Hwyl (pronounced hoo-il) is a Welsh word meaning a ship's canvas. The expression "catching the hwyl" referred to a preacher caught up in enthusiastic passion as he preached - like a ship driven by sails filled with the wind. This element in preaching helps both the preacher himself and the congregation. We must not preach as if "in the doldrums" - like a ship with no wind in its sails. We need to catch the hwyl and preach with fervency.

In his 1910 Yale Lectures on Preaching, Charles Jefferson observed, "The whole world brightens when a man appears able to unfold *in syllables of fire* the unsearchable riches of Christ." [emphasis mine]

Earnestness, passion, fervency. How can we ensure that our preaching has this essential quality? The following chapters explain principles that will help to develop and maintain fervency in preaching.

Chapter 1
Preach God's Truth

"Preaching has fallen on evil days because the sermon is regarded as just another form of human speech, rather than a special genre. The preacher is just another Christian without any special authority; the pulpit is just another platform or lectern - sometimes (even worse) it is a private stage. And when preachers believe this way, they lack the courage to speak with authority and to bless." These words were written by Joseph Parker, 19th century pastor of London's large City Temple. Unfortunately, the "evil days" Parker argued preaching had fallen on are still with us. Personally, I think they have grown worse.

Contemporary preaching is too often accompanied by disclaimers and apologies. Tentative preachers either avoid certain controversial topics addressed in Scripture, amend the Bible's teaching on those subjects, or speak with hesitancy out of fear of offending the feelings of the listeners.

D. Martin Lloyd-Jones wrote that the preacher "should never give the impression that he is speaking by their leave as it were; he should not be tentatively putting forward certain suggestions and ideas... He is a man under commission and under authority. He is an ambassador, and he should be aware of his authority."

When a preacher is mindful of the fact that he is under a great commission to preach God's truth, he will preach with authority - and he will preach with fervency.

I. Appreciating Inspiration

When I was a college student, on one occasion, I visited relatives out of state and went to church with them on Sunday morning. Their church was part of a different denomination than the one I usually attended, and I learned it had a different emphasis. For the most part, the order of service was similar to that with which I was familiar. There was hymn singing, prayer, and an offering. Then the minister stood behind the pulpit to preach. But there was something very odd about his presentation - at least it was very odd to me. In his sermon he talked about various subjects ranging from politics to social problems. But he never cited the Scripture. I do remember he quoted from *National Geographic*. But he never opened the Bible.

Paul told Timothy, "preach the word" (II Tim. 4:2). What is this word that Timothy and all Christian preachers are to preach? The answer is found back in II Timothy 3:16. The word preachers are to preach is the inspired written revelation of God, the Bible.

II Timothy 3:16 is perhaps the most important single verse about the nature and function of the Bible. It says, "All scripture is given by inspiration of God..." The word "inspiration" does not mean the same thing as if a person were to say that Beethoven was an inspired composer, or an athlete played inspired ball. It does not mean a sudden burst of creativity or a surge of energy. "Inspiration" comes from a Greek word, *theopneustos*, which means "God-breathed." This word is made up of two parts: The first is *theos*, meaning God. This is commonly understood. For instance, *theo*logy is the study of God or the things pertaining to God. The second is *pneo* which means to breathe or to blow. This shows up in some English words. For example, a *pneu*matic drill is an air-powered drill.

It is absolutely correct for a Christian to refer to the Bible as the word of God. It is the revelation of God in written form. It is what God has to say because it is what God has said. It is not inspired in certain places and not in others. It is "all scripture" that is given by inspiration of God. It is not just the concepts or ideas that are inspired. It is the very words that are inspired. It includes, as Jesus said, the "jot and tittle" (Mt. 5:18) - every verb, every letter. The Holy Spirit guided certain men to write what they wrote. Their own personalities are reflected in their writings. Yet, as they wrote, the Spirit of God led them in what to write and preserved them from error and omission as they wrote. This makes the Bible uniquely the word of God.

The Bible is inspired, inerrant, and is therefore also authoritative. Appreciating the nature of Scripture ought to energize the preacher as he preaches the Bible.

Joseph Parker said, "Where there is no authority there can be no appeal. Men ought to have the courage of their inspiration."

When the coach talks, his team listens. When a general speaks, his troops give undivided attention. When a physician gives his diagnosis, the patient concentrates. When the president addresses the nation, regularly scheduled programming is interrupted. In each instance, the person speaking has authority. There is no authority greater than that of God Almighty. When a preacher delivers a message from the Bible, he stands before his listeners as God's ambassador bringing a message from on high. When the preacher explains a passage of Scripture and exhorts his hearers to believe it and apply it to their lives, he can say, "Thus saith the Lord!" This fact ought to embolden the preacher's delivery. It ought to endow him with fervency.

The people marveled at Jesus Christ's preaching because he did not speak as other men such as the scribes did. He spoke with authority (Matt. 7:29). When the preacher understands that his message is not his own, but is in fact the word of God, he can speak even as Christ spoke, with authority. Speaking with authority encourages the preacher to speak uninhibited - with fervency.

II. Understanding the Intention

II Timothy 3:16 tells us another vital truth about the Bible. It not only says that "all scripture is given by inspiration of God." It also says that it "is profitable." The word profitable means helpful, useful, beneficial.

Ever since the "battle for the Bible" erupted in the 19th century with modernists challenging the inspiration and inerrancy of Scripture, conservatives have defended the Bible, that "it is in truth, the word of God" (I Thess. 2:13). However, in preaching about the Bible, some have neglected the purpose of the Bible. God did not inspire the Bible to be a theological novelty. It is not an ancient artifact to be admired at a distance. It is not some sort of Christian talisman to be revered and discussed. It is a divine revelation from God to be understood and applied practically. It is a helpful tool to be employed. It is useful and to be used. It gives answers to our questions, comfort for our sorrows, correction for our errors, guidance for our way. It provides essential instruction for life here and hereafter. Someone said of the Bible, "Herein is found the best way of living, the noblest way of suffering, and the most comfortable way of dying." The Bible is essential.

> *When the intention of Scripture, as well as the nature of Scripture, is understood and appreciated by the preacher, it ought to influence the way he preaches.*

The preacher must approach the pulpit with this in mind. People need the Word of God. They need to have the Bible preached to them. When the intention of Scripture, as well as the nature of Scripture, is understood and appreciated by the preacher, it ought to influence the way he preaches. It ought to stir up his delivery. It ought to encourage fervency in preaching.

III. Revitalizing the Communication

The prophet Jeremiah did not seek out the office of prophet. Instead, he resisted it. When the calling of God came to him, he protested, "Ah, Lord God! Behold, I cannot speak, for I am a child" (Jer. 1:6). He was young and inexperienced. As such, he thought he lacked the credibility and capability to preach to the people of Judah. He did not feel that he was up to the job. But the Lord offered him two words of assurance: "I am with thee..." (v. 8), and "I have put my words in thy mouth" (v. 9).

These two encouragements live on for the contemporary gospel preacher. The Lord promised us His presence when He said, "Lo, I am with you alway..." (Matt. 28:20). And He authorized us to speak on His behalf when He said, "He that heareth you heareth me" (Lk. 10:16). We do not have the gift of prophecy like Jeremiah, receiving and proclaiming new revelation from God. But we have God's revelation, nonetheless, preserved in Scripture. So, when a preacher faithfully

11

preaches the Bible, he can and should speak with the bold authority of the prophets of old. He is not speaking his own words, but the word of God.

The apostle Peter wrote, "If any man speak, let him speak as the oracles of God" (I Pet. 4:11). D. Edmond Hiebert explains this as meaning, "He should be conscious that what he says is God's message for the occasion... he is not just giving his own opinion but, under the leadership of the Spirit, is delivering God's word."

The apostle Paul understood this. He thanked God in I Thessalonians 2:13 that the people who made up this early church received the message he brought to them, "not as the word of men, but as it is in truth, the word of God..." It wasn't Paul's word. It was God's word. What enabled Paul to speak the gospel boldly in the face of threats and persecution? He was not delivering his own message. His preaching was backed by the authority of the Almighty. He was preaching God's truth.

When my children were young, on one occasion my older son was outside playing baseball. I wished to speak to him, so I sent his younger brother to tell him to come inside. The younger brother returned to me a few minutes later to tell me, "He won't listen to me." I sent him a second time with the following instructions: "You tell him his father says to come inside." This time the older brother complied. Why? Authority. Little brothers don't usually boss their big brothers around, and older brothers don't normally feel compelled to listen to their younger siblings. But every child ought to listen to his father.

Webster defines authority as "the right to command or make final decisions." God has such a right. When the preacher communicates what God has said he is not speaking his own ideas or expressing his own will. He is a herald bearing the proclamation of a king.

Every Bible preacher should preach with the conviction that his message is authoritative and worthy of hearing. When a preacher communicates what God has said, he speaks with all the authority of heaven. Preaching God's truth, rather than man's opinion, ought to liberate the preacher from intimidation and hesitancy. The conviction that what is being communicated is the authoritative word of God ought to bring fervency to preaching.

FORMULA:
Authority → Conviction → Fervency

Chapter 2
Preach an Empowered Truth

In Acts 4, the apostles Peter and John were arrested, assaulted, and further threatened to cease their preaching. Following their release, the two apostles met with a group of disciples. They told of their experiences and then led in a season of prayer. The effect was the disciples were "filled with the Holy Ghost, and they spake the word of God with boldness" (Acts 4:31). The word translated "boldness" is rendered elsewhere in the New Testament, "openly," "plainly," "with confidence." Although there had been violent persecution and threats of more, these believers openly shared the gospel with freedom and confidence. How did this happen? How can a preacher deliver a message with boldness and fervency instead of with reticence and intimidation? He can do so by the power of the Holy Spirit.

Perry and Strubhar called the Holy Spirit the preacher's "indispensible partner in the proclamation of the gospel." They further observed, "The scriptural analogies regarding the Holy Spirit speak to this point. In John 3, He is likened to wind that stirs. In Acts 2, He is likened to fire that purifies. In Isaiah 61, He is likened to oil that invigorates. In Revelation 22, He is likened to water that refreshes."

How desperately the church and the wider world needs preaching that stirs, purifies, invigorates, and refreshes!

How can a preacher deliver messages that have this kind of effect? How can a preacher preach with the power of the Holy Spirit?

I. The Holy Spirit is the Producer of the Preacher's Message

The apostle Peter stressed the role of the Holy Spirit in the writing of the Bible. "Holy men of God" did indeed write the Bible, but they did so as they were "moved" or borne along by the Holy Spirit (II Pet. 1:21). Peter did not deny that men wrote the Scriptures. Rather, he affirmed that they did so guided and controlled by the Holy Spirit. Moses, David, John, and Paul were penmen of inspired Scripture. But it is not incorrect to say that the Holy Ghost authored the Bible.

Ephesians 5:18 commands the believer "to be filled with the Spirit." The effect of this filling is described in v. 19, "speaking to yourselves in psalms and hymns... giving thanks always for all things... submitting yourselves one to another..." Our attitudes, our reaction to circumstances, our relationships to others are all impacted positively by the Spirit's filling.

An interesting parallel passage is found in the third chapter of the Colossian letter. There the imperative appears to be completely different: "Let the word of Christ dwell in you richly..." (3:16). However the effect is exactly the same: "Teaching and admonishing one another is psalms and hymns... giving thanks to God... submit yourselves..." (3:16b-18). This is not coincidental.

If the Holy Spirit is the author of the word of God, then to have your mind and heart directed by the word of God is in a sense to be controlled by the Holy Spirit!

The preacher needs to trust that he is preaching what the Spirit has revealed and he needs to limit his preaching to that which the Spirit has revealed. In doing so, he will be delivering a message that ultimately comes from the Spirit of God. This way he will enjoy the power of the Holy Spirit on his ministry.

Early in his ministry, 19th century evangelist Dwight Moody was taught a lesson by another evangelist that revolutionized Moody's later work. Harry Moorehouse told Moody, "Learn to preach God's words instead of your own. He will make you a great power for good." Moody took Moorehouse's admonition to heart. Although he had no formal training, Moody prepared and preached sermons that were saturated with Scripture. As a result, his ministry was marked by great power.

II. The Holy Spirit is the Penetrator of the Preacher's Understanding

It is essential to remember that the matter of sermon preparation and delivery is far more than an academic exercise. A thorough knowledge of linguistics, history, theology, logic, and rhetoric do not make a preacher. Study is important. However, there is a distinctly spiritual aspect to the matter of preaching that cannot be accounted for through scholarly labor alone. Prayer and meditation must also be a part of sermon preparation.

The Psalmist prayed, "Open thou mine eyes, that I may behold wondrous things out of thy law" (Ps. 119:18). He was not praying for a miraculous infusion of knowledge in grammar and vocabulary. He was asking for something more.

II Corinthians 2:14 is often misunderstood. When Paul wrote that "the natural man receiveth not the things of the Spirit of God," he was not saying that unbelievers were incapable of comprehending the plain meaning of the Bible. A man who is able to read with understanding can read the Bible just as he reads any other literature. What he cannot do is appreciate its significance in his life.

That is the work of the Holy Spirit. Theologians call this special work of the Holy Spirit "illumination."

The Holy Spirit was sent by Christ into the world after His ascension "to reprove [or convince] the world of sin, and of righteousness, and of judgment" (Jn. 16:8). When a man without faith in Christ, upon hearing the gospel, ascertains his own sinfulness, his need of righteousness, and his accountability to God, we say he has come under the conviction of the Holy Spirit. This is correct. When a sinner recognizes his spiritual need, realizes that his need is met in Christ, and then embraces Christ as Savior and Lord, this is the work of the Holy Spirit (I Cor. 12:3b).

The Holy Spirit was also sent to work in the lives of the saints. One of His ministries to the people of God is teaching. Jesus said of the Holy Spirit, "... he shall teach you all things, and bring all things to your remembrance whatsoever I have said unto you" (Jn. 14:26). Again, the Spirit does not teach us how to read. He helps believers appreciate the significance of God's word, and He helps them make practical application of it in their lives.

"How shall they hear without a preacher?" (Rom. 10:14). The Holy Spirit does not work in a vacuum. He uses means to accomplish His work. He uses preachers. When a preacher delivers the word of God to Christians and unbelievers alike, he must do so utterly dependent upon the power of the Holy Spirit. The Spirit opens the mind of the preacher to understand the word so that he may deliver it to others. It is the Holy Spirit Who, in the study, helps the preacher appreciate the practical significance of the word and its application for those under his care. It is this work of the Spirit that allows a preacher to deliver sermons with fresh and vital devotional value - sermons beneficial to even mature

Christians who may have studied the preacher's text countless times before.

III. The Holy Spirit is the Enabler of the Preacher's Declaration

A preacher may doubt that he can impact people's lives through his preaching because he is lacking in communication skills. He knows he is not a wordsmith. He does not possess a flair for the dramatic, that "gift of gab." Neither did the apostle Paul.

Some may imagine the great apostle to the Gentiles as an imposing physical presence, standing like King Saul, head and shoulders above the rest of the crowd. Some imagine him preaching with spellbinding eloquence like the prophet Ezekiel whose delivery was likened to a lovely song sung by a man with a pleasant voice (Ez. 33:32). Paul was neither of these. Some observed of Paul that "his bodily presence is weak, and his speech contemptible" (II Cor. 10:10). While the critic's assessment of Paul may have been exaggerated, apparently, from a human standpoint, he wasn't much to see or hear. Still the Bible says that he preached with power (I Thess. 1:5). His power was not the persuasive influence of human reason or personality. It was not the power of flowery oratory. It was the power of the Holy Spirit.

It is the Holy Spirit who convicts, converts, comforts, corrects, and builds up the people of God into the fullness of the stature of Christ. The matter of preaching must be approached with this clearly in mind.

"What does it mean to be filled with the Holy Spirit?" I was asked this question years ago by a seasoned pastor during a workshop I was teaching at a Bible conference. I was a little surprised, not by the question, but by who asked it. I assumed a man with many years of experience in the gospel ministry would understand this important concept. However, there is a great deal of confusion about the Holy Spirit and His work. Although the command to be filled with the Spirit is an important command, it is widely misunderstood.

The context in which this phrase is found in Ephesians 5:18 actually explains what is meant by Spirit filling. Paul writes, "Be not drunk with wine wherein is excess, but be filled with the Spirit." Drunkenness is obviously a serious problem and forbidding it, an important prohibition. However, this command against drunkenness does not stand alone. Paul was not writing a list of unrelated exhortations. There is a deliberate contrast here between drunkenness and Spirit filling. When a person is drunk, in modern vernacular sometimes we say he is "under the influence." Alcohol can induce people to do and say things they would not normally - usually destructive things. The term "wherein is excess" has also been translated "dissipation," "debauchery," "recklessness." Just as alcohol can influence an individual to reckless, destructive behavior, the Holy Spirit can influence an individual to godly, constructive behavior. To be filled with the Spirit means to be under the influence of the Holy Spirit. The result is to be led to do what otherwise would or could not be done.

In Luke 4:28 we read that men "filled with wrath" attempted to kill Jesus Christ. Their wrath led them to attempt murder. In contrast, when a man is filled with the Holy Spirit, he will be led by the Spirit to attempt and achieve good for the glory of God and the benefit of others.

An otherwise timid man can stand before a congregation - even an unfriendly, unwelcoming crowd - and preach God's truth with passion.

A preacher, filled with the Holy Spirit - under the influence of the Holy Spirit - can preach boldly and with power. An otherwise timid man can stand before a congregation - even an unfriendly, unwelcoming crowd - and preach God's truth with passion.

On the night in which the Savior was betrayed, the apostle Peter denied Christ when he was confronted about his association with Him. Forty days later, this same frightened fisherman stood on Pentecost and preached to a multitude. The difference? Jesus said "Ye shall receive power after that the Holy Ghost is come upon you" (Acts 1:8). Filled with the Spirit of God, Peter lifted up his voice and fearlessly proclaimed the resurrection of Jesus Christ.

The gift of the apostle has passed off the scene. The gift of the Holy Spirit abides. Preacher, yield yourself completely to the Lord. Trust God as you preach. Emptied of self, completely dependent upon God, filled with the Holy Spirit, you can speak the word of God with power. You can preach with fervency.

FORMULA:
Faith → Filling → Fervency

Chapter 3
Preach a Singular Truth

Sometimes sermons fail because they say too little. Peter was told by the Lord, "Feed my lambs" (Jn. 21:15). He was not told to give them a light snack. The preacher should always endeavor to place before his listeners a full helping of the word of God.

It is also true that some sermons fail because they say too much. You may wonder, how is that possible? A sermon can say too much when the preacher delivers meat to souls only mature enough to take in milk. The Bible affirms that there are some things young believers are just not capable of receiving (I Cor. 2:2; Heb. 5:12). Know your congregation and preach accordingly.

A sermon can say too much when the preacher refers to concepts and employs words with which the congregation is unfamiliar. The divine master should keep in mind that while he may have attended seminary and spent years in the company of doctors of theology, his listeners have not. A preacher should always explain concepts, define terms, and use a vocabulary familiar to his listeners. As Billy Sunday said, "keep the cookies on the lower shelf." Preach to the congregation as they are, not as you are.

A sermon can say too much when it takes longer to preach the sermon than the congregation's capacity to listen. When a preacher speaks far beyond people's ability to sit attentively, he has said too much. Blessed is the preacher who knows when to finish.

A sermon can say too much when it says many things instead of one thing. Charles Spurgeon observed, "One thought fixed in the mind will be better than fifty thoughts made to flit across the ear. One tenpenny nail driven home and clenched will be more useful than a score of tintacks loosely fixed, to be pulled out again in an hour." The congregation will not profit as much by a sermon that communicates several truths as by a sermon that focuses on a singular truth. As well, it is far easier and more natural for a preacher to be fervent in his delivery if he is attempting to make one point instead of making many.

I. The Meaning

Every student of homiletics is taught the basic parts of a sermon: text, topic or theme, introduction, body, and conclusion. The theme is the central idea of a sermon. However, every sermon ought to have more than just a theme. It must have a proposition. By strict definition, a proposition is a statement to be upheld; a declarative sentence. In preaching, a proposition is a concise propositional statement of God's truth. This has been called "the controlling assertion," or "the sermon in one sentence."

In his helpful book, *Preaching with Confidence*, James Daane argued, "Every sermon must say one thing, and one thing only; and this one thing must be capable of statement in a single sentence. The more points a sermon tries to drive home, the less it drives home. A many pointed sermon makes no point."

In addition to the five basic parts of a sermon, I contend that ministerial students ought to be taught a necessary sixth part. Right after the theme and before the introduction there should be a clearly stated proposition. Including this element in the sermon can make the difference between a dull lecture in theology and the passionate proclamation of God's truth.

For example, using the latter part of James 5:16 as a text - "the effectual fervent prayer of a righteous man availeth much." - a preacher may construct a sermon with the theme, "fervent prayer." What might be a proposition for a sermon on this text with this theme? How about, "Fervent prayer gets results." This communicates the point of the sermon. It summarizes the entire sermon in a single sentence. Stating that proposition clearly with a heart-felt energy is preaching. Everything the preacher says in his sermon then is either illustration, explanation, or application of this declarative sentence.

Here are some sample propositions that come directly from Scripture:

- You cannot escape the consequences of your sin (Num. 32:23).
- God cares for you (I Pet. 5:7).
- You can have peace in the midst of trials (Phil. 4:7).
- No one can be saved apart from faith in Jesus Christ (Acts 4:12).
- You need to yield your life completely to God (Rom. 12:1).
- God wants to use you to be a blessing to others (I Cor. 12:7).

Each of these statements is a concise declaration of biblical truth that can be preached effectively for the benefit of others.

II. The Distinctives

First, propositional preaching is not compound. It is singular in substance and focus.

II Timothy 2:1-4 says, "I exhort therefore that first of all, supplications, prayers, intercessions, and giving of thanks be made for all men... for this is good and acceptable before God who will have all men to be saved..." Using this text, a theme of prayer and a burden for souls might be developed. However, that would be a poor theme because it is not singular. There are two themes there. A better theme would be, "prayer for souls." And what proposition could be made from this text? "Praying for souls is important" or "Christians ought to pray that people will be saved."

Second, propositional preaching is not broad. It is concise.

A preacher may select a familiar text such as John 3:16 and prepare a message with salvation as its theme. However, that would be far too general. The topic of salvation is very broad and cannot be sufficiently covered in a single sermon. For this text, "The love of God in salvation" would be more specific. The proposition then could be, "You need to know about the love of God in salvation."

Is propositional preaching necessarily shallow, without much content? Is it just preparing and preaching one point sermons without any outline? Certainly not.

Again, taking John 3:16 as the text, and "The love of God" as the theme, and "You need to know about the love of God" as the proposition, the outline could look like this:

I. The Declaration of God's Love
("For God so loved the world...")
   "God has told you that He loves you."

II. The Display of God's Love
("...that he gave his only begotten son...")
   "God has showed you that He loves you."

III. The Desire of God's Love
("...that whosoever believeth in him should not perish, but have everlasting life.")

"God so loves you that He wants you to be saved."

Employing the same text, John 3:16, the preacher could prepare and deliver a sermon on everlasting life. The proposition, "God wants you to have everlasting life." The outline:

I. The Possibility of Everlasting Life

    A. The Availability
    ("whosoever believeth...")

    B. The Simplicity
    ("believeth")

II. The Protection of Everlasting Life

    A. Its Contrast
    ("should not perish")

    B. Its Cost
    ("his only begotten son")

III. The Procurement of Everlasting Life

    A. Its Duration
    ("everlasting")

    B. Its Delight
    ("life")

John 3:16 may seem to be an easy and obvious text. Does this approach to preaching work on more complicated passages such as Old Testament narratives? Absolutely. Take I Kings 17:2-7 where Elijah is sustained by ravens at the brook Cherith. The proposition is, "Trust God to provide for His people (or better, for you)."

I. The Promise of God's Provision
("I have commanded the ravens to feed thee...")
You should trust God to provide for you because He has promised to do so.

II. The Place of God's Provision
("I have commanded the ravens to feed thee there.")
You should trust God to provide for you in whatever place He has appointed.

III. The Patience of God's Provision
(v. 7, "... the brook dried up.")
You should trust God to provide for you even when circumstances appear impossible.

It is important to notice that every point in the sermon outline states, explains, or defends the proposition. The points in a sermon outline are like pillars that support the roof of a building. The roof is the proposition. Each pillar holds it up. It would be strange to see a building with supporting pillars holding up the roof, but also with one or two pillars standing off alone holding up nothing. That happens sometimes in preaching. Some sermons are prepared and delivered with points holding up nothing. They simply stand off by themselves. Such points are not parallel. These points may express truth, but they distract from the main truth. It is hard for a congregation to follow such preaching. It is difficult for the preacher to be focused and fervent when he is dealing with different themes and different propositions in a single sermon.

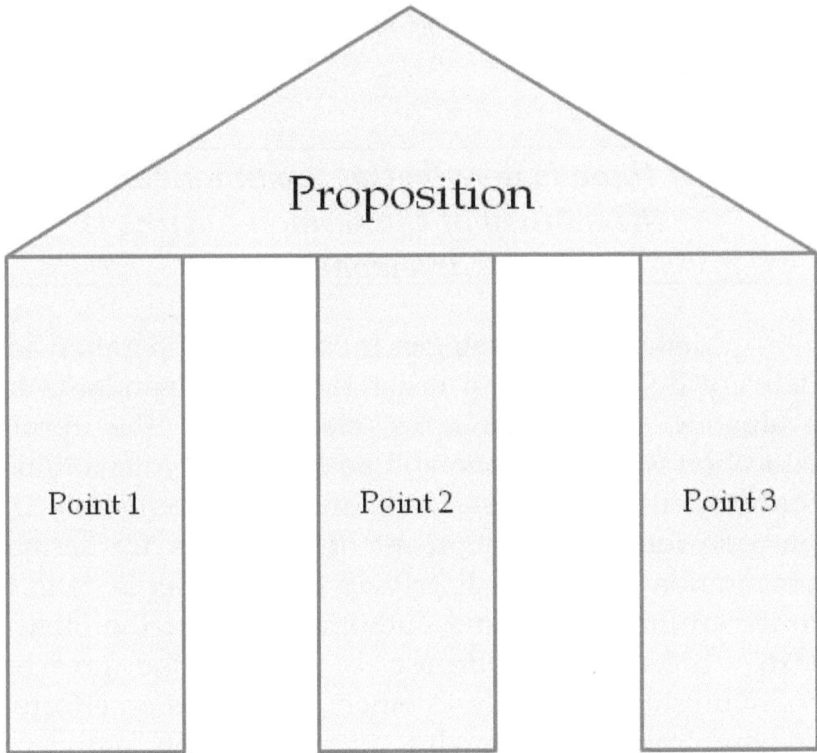

```
                    /\
                   /  \
                  /    \
                 /      \
                /        \
               /          \
              / Proposition \
             /_____ \
            |  |   |   |   |  |
            |  |   |   |   |  |
            |  |   |   |   |  |
            |Point 1| |Point 2| |Point 3|
            |  |   |   |   |  |
            |__|   |___|   |__|
```

Some may argue that preaching propositionally may be fine for topical messages, but it is inconsistent with expository or exegetical preaching that examines the details of a text. Actually, preaching expositionally does not mean a sermon has to be a running commentary. I would urge preachers to avoid that approach. While I am certain my view would elicit strong objections from some, I believe preaching a running commentary tends to make a sermon tedious and easy to forget. It is because some expositors do not preach propositionally that they tend to be academic and wearisome in their delivery. A sermon should be less like a shish kebab and more like a 12 oz. steak. A sermon should not be a list of unrelated ideas. It should be singular in thought and focus. Expositional preaching can and should be propositional.

III. The Values

If there is no effective communication, the quality of the sermon outline is irrelevant.

Methods and strategies for sermon preparation and delivery do not exist in order to provide standards for evaluation in a homiletics class. After the formal education is over, no one will be critiquing your outlines for homiletical exactness. (At least no one should be!) The purpose for the development of principles for sermon preparation is, first of all, to help the preacher be faithful to the inspired truth and authorial intent of the biblical text. Second, the purpose is to help the preacher communicate effectively to others. If there is no effective communication, the quality of the sermon outline is irrelevant.

In keeping with this important subject of fervency in preaching, one of the great values of propositional preaching - preaching a singular truth - is that it helps create and maintain attention to the sermon.

Even earnest listeners can be distracted or daydream during the course of a message. By being focused on communicating one great truth, the preacher will have more concentration and more fervency in his delivery. This will help command and hold the attention of the listeners.

As strange as it may seem, sometimes the person whose attention is lost during the course of a sermon is the preacher himself. How can this be? The man behind the pulpit is not immune to distractions, such as a crying baby, a low-flying plane, or even his own wandering thoughts. Occasionally a preacher will "chase a rabbit trail." He will go off on a tangent for a moment and forget where he was in his message. He may become caught up in the details or the drama of an illustration and actually lose track of the point he was attempting to illustrate! Every man who has long experience preaching will acknowledge that this happens. By preaching propositionally, the preacher who loses his own attention will always know how to get back on track in his sermon. He simply returns to the proposition. Restate it, and then go on preaching.

In addition to attention, a second great value in preaching a singular truth is retention. As regrettable as it may be, the fact is few people in a congregation are fully attentive and fully engaged during an entire sermon. If a preacher is delivering a message with a single proposition, and a listener hears only a portion of the sermon, he will still have a grasp of the big idea the preacher is trying to communicate. Following a church service, ask a random member of the congregation what the preacher just preached about. (Actually, don't do this if you are a preacher. You will probably be discouraged by the answer!) Sometimes people who have sat through a church service honestly have no idea what the preacher just spent the past half hour talking about! But if the preacher is preaching one truth - repeating it, illustrating it, explaining it, and applying it - it is far more likely that members of the congregation will go away remembering what it was the preacher was preaching.

Focusing on a singular truth, concentrating and being burdened to communicate that one idea, the preacher will be more fervent and passionate in his delivery. The Savior's attention was fixed on one thing - accomplishing His redemptive work. He said, "How am I straitened til it be accomplished!" (Lk. 12:50) As the preacher approaches the pulpit his attention needs to be fixed on one truth. And he must be straitened till it be preached! Preaching a singular truth will lead the preacher to preach with fervency.

FORMULA:
Focus → Concentration → Fervency

Chapter 4
Preach a Timeless Truth

While I attended seminary, I supported myself and my new wife by working at a textile mill. It was a hot, dirty job. However, it not only paid the bills, it also taught me a great deal about life. I met some very interesting people at the mill. One of them was an enormous man - perhaps the largest human being I have ever seen. He must have stood seven feet tall, and he was nearly as wide as he was tall. I am certain, based upon the way he talked, that he was not very well educated. But he was a friendly man and a devoted Christian. Once, while I was in the break room eating lunch, this giant of a man was sitting at the next table talking with another worker. The fellow he was talking with was old, short, and had a green *Pioneer Seed* cap resting on his balding head. Apparently, they were discussing religion. The older man seemed to be taunting the big man with questions.

"You think you know a lot about the Bible, huh?"

"Well," the big man replied, "I tries to read from it every day."

"Well, if you know so much about the Bible, who's the strongest man in the world?"

The big man hesitated before finally answering, "Who's the strongest man in the world? How am I supposed to know who's the strongest man in the world?"

The man in the green baseball cap then raised his voice, "You don't know so much about the Bible! You don't even know who the strongest man in the world is! Samson! Samson's the strongest man in the world!"

The big man started to laugh. "A lot you know! How can he be the strongest man in the world? Samson's dead!"

Their argument ended there.

"Samson's dead!" There is a valuable lesson in this seemingly ridiculous statement that every preacher should remember.

The Bible is not simply a history book about people from long ago who lived in a culture very much foreign to our own. It is a timeless book, as pertinent to people living today as it has ever been. The Bible is not about Samson. It is not about Noah, David, or Paul. These people are all dead. It is about God, and it is about you and me, and that is how it must be preached.

Several years ago a popular magazine conducted a survey among high school students to determine their preferences in academic subjects. The survey showed that the least favorite subject among young people was history. (I would have answered mathematics!)

Some preachers preach sermons that are little more than history lessons. Then they wonder why their listeners are bored or uninterested. It is difficult for most people to be enthusiastic about names, dates, and places from long ago. Preaching is not about the past. It is about the present and the future. Preaching is supposed to be the communication of timeless truth that impacts the lives of the listeners. This helps make preaching passionate.

Someone once said, "Great preaching should always be in the present tense."

Haddon Robinson, in his seminal book on expository preaching, *Biblical Preaching*, wrote, "An expository preacher trades a sword for a butter knife when he sounds like a lecturer in ancient history discussing a saga from the long ago and far away."

34

Preaching timeless truth has certain values that encourage and enable fervency. The preacher needs to preach timeless truths that are:

I. Permanent

Genesis 22:1-14 is a wonderful preaching text. It tells the stirring story of God asking Abraham to offer his son Isaac in sacrifice. A sermon on this text might have as its theme, "The testing of Abraham's faith." However, this would be a very poor theme. Why? Because, like Samson, Abraham is dead. For some, it might be interesting to learn about a bedouin and his son who lived some four thousand years ago. However, most people have little or no interest in ancient near eastern history.

A far better theme would be, "The testing of the believer's faith." Or how about, "The testing of the Christian's faith." Sure, Abraham's faith was tested, but sometimes our faith is tested as well. What is true about Abraham's experience that is also true about our experience? The answer to that question is what is to be preached. The history is background. The timeless truth is the message.

What the preacher is to proclaim is not the events of history, but the timeless truths that impacted people in the Bible, and still impact the lives of people today.

In I Corinthians 10, the apostle Paul cites the events surrounding the wilderness wandering of the Israelites. He refers to their sin and subsequent divine judgment. Then he makes contemporary application to the

Corinthian believers to whom he was penning this letter. "We should not lust... neither be ye idolaters... neither let us commit fornication..." He makes several practical moral and spiritual admonitions based on the experience of people who lived many centuries prior. How did he do this? In v. 11, Paul explains, "Now all these things happened unto them for examples: and they are written for our admonition, upon whom the ends of the world are come." The events recorded in the Bible are there to illustrate and communicate timeless truth that has practical value for the present generation. Again, what the preacher is to proclaim is not the events of history, but the timeless truths that impacted people in the Bible, and still impact the lives of people today.

Delivering relevant, timeless messages lends itself to fervency far more than reciting the events of ancient history.

II. Principial

What is "principial?" I did not invent this word in some sort of misguided zeal to alliterate my points. Years ago I heard a preacher named Doug McLaughlin use this word to identify a necessary component of good preaching. He either gets the credit or the blame for its use here.

Saying that preaching timeless truth is principial means that it communicates principles. That makes for effective preaching. That also encourages fervency. What is a principle? It is not the man whose office I visited frequently when I was in grade school. That is the principal. A principle is a rule or guideline by which an individual directs his life. It is a general truth with broad application.

Which of the following statements is a principle?

1) The Bible contains sixty-six books.
2) Go for all the gusto you can get.
3) The sky is blue.

Actually, only the second one is a principle. It is not a good principle, certainly, but it is a principle. It is a rule or guideline by which some people govern their actions. The other two are statements of truth, but they are not principles.

The statement, "The sky is blue," is admittedly a timeless truth. The sky did not used to be another color, and it will still be blue tomorrow. But this is not a principle. It is not a general truth by which we can guide our lives.

Even great biblical themes and theological realities need to be presented in principial form for effective preaching. "God created the world" is true. It is a timeless truth. It is true today, just as it was true when the Lord walked the earth two thousand years ago. But even this great assertion *by itself* is inadequate for preaching. To preach it, it must be made principial. The Bible says, "God created the heaven and the earth" (Gen. 1:1). "God created the world, and is deserving of our worship." "God created the world, and we are accountable to Him." "God created the world, and we are dependent upon Him." Now it is a timeless truth presented in a way that that includes general truth with broad application. This makes it relevant and useful, which is precisely what God intended His word to be - "profitable" (II Tim. 3:16).

III. Practical

Before explaining this third point about timeless preaching, a disclaimer must be made. In much of contemporary gospel ministry there is an over-emphasis on cultural relevance. Many church growth experts tell preachers that they need to study their culture nearly as much as they need to study the Scripture. And they are told by church marketing gurus that their preaching must be tailored to suit the culture or risk being ignored as irrelevant.

A. W. Tozer wisely observed, "God's word is true whether we believe it or not. Human unbelief cannot alter the character of God." I think it can also be said, God's word is relevant whether we realize it or not. The fact that God said something makes it relevant, whether or not we understand it as such. God's truth is what we need even if we do not realize it.

A college professor of mine named Jesse Boyd once told the story of an old man who lay dying in his bed from a long illness. With weak and trembling voice he asked his son, "Bring the Bible."

"Where should I read?" his son asked.

"Anywhere. It's all God's word."

The younger man, not as familiar with the Bible as his aged father, opened the Bible toward the middle and began to read a verse. Then he stopped. He had opened to the first chapter of I Chronicles where a lengthy genealogy begins.

"You don't want to hear this. Let me turn to another passage."

His father urged him, "No, it's all God's word. Read. Read."

So, he read. He read exhaustively the hundreds of hard to pronounce names that make up the first nine chapters of I Chronicles. When he finished, the old man stirred himself, drew a deep breath and smiled.

"And the Lord God knew them all!"

Even from this seemingly obscure text of Scripture, the truth of God's word provided comfort to this dying man's heart.

God's word is practical. It is what people need in any circumstance of life. Recognizing that the timeless truth of the Bible is what people need most should energize the preacher in his work. It should encourage passion in the pulpit.

In my pastoral ministry I preach twice every Sunday. I usually have a systematic series of sermons going in one service, and then I preach unrelated texts in the other. There is a reason for this approach. First, I select texts and topics that I perceive are important to the congregation. I have heard some preachers argue that they exclusively preach sermon series because that is the only proper way to preach. I disagree. A physician examines his patient and applies treatments based on what he diagnoses. A pastor ought to do likewise. I am not suggesting that he should take people's individual personal problems to the pulpit. However, he should address the congregation's present challenges and deficiencies in his preaching. He also should not give undue attention to matters that are not particularly pertinent. I heard a homiletics professor jokingly tell his students not to preach on dating standards in the nursing home service. This may sound absurd. Yet, sometimes a pastor lingers long in a sermon series completely unrelated to major spiritual concerns in the church. A congregation grieving over an unexpected death in their midst should not be greeted on Sunday by a sermon on stewardship. They should hear a message about comfort, grace, or heaven. The preacher can appear unaware or uncaring if he ignores matters that are demanding his attention.

But I also engage in series preaching because often I find that it leads me to preach on subjects I might not think of on my own. It also leads me to address issues of need of which I am unaware. Often a series has brought me to an obscure text I would never select on my own. But the result was insightful, practical preaching! God is omniscient, and I believe His providence is at work in my pulpit ministry.

Recognizing the immediate practical value of some of my sermons and believing in the spiritual value of all of them energizes my preaching.

Richard Cecil said, "To love to preach is one thing. To love those to whom you preach is another." We should care about people and want to meet their needs from the Bible. Go from people's needs to the Scripture or go from the Scripture to people's needs. Jesus told Peter, "Feed my lambs."

Our love for our listeners, coupled with the assurance that God's timeless truth is precisely what they need most should stimulate our work in the pulpit and give it fervency.

FORMULA:
Relevance → Concern → Fervency

Chapter 5
Preach a Living Truth

In I Timothy 4:16, the apostle Paul wrote to a young preacher, "Take heed unto thyself and unto the doctrine [or teaching] ..." Paul here reminded Timothy that while the message is vitally important, the messenger also matters. There are two diligent considerations here for the young preacher: The second is doctrine. The first is the preacher himself.

I. Diligent Considerations

In I Timothy 4:16, the term "take heed" comes from a Greek word meaning "to get a grip on," "to hold onto," or "to pay careful attention to." Paul told Timothy in essence, "get a grip on your personal spiritual condition and on your teaching."

It is essential that the preacher take himself in hand.

A great preacher must first be a great Christian.

When I was studying for the ministry, occasionally in chapel or in the classroom I would hear a statement - some pithy saying - that struck me as particularly profound and important. I would write these statements in the flyleaf of my Bible to help me remember them. Because the Bible I used in college and seminary is old and tattered, I no longer use it. However, every once in a while, I take this old Bible down from the shelf, turn to this page, and rehearse these statements in my mind. One that stands out to me is simple and obvious yet is very significant. "A great preacher must first be a great Christian." No educational attainment, no oratorical skill, no exegetical insight will compensate for want of a close walk with Christ.

In his classic on preaching, *How to Prepare Sermons*, William Evans observed, "The preacher must be himself, his best self, his consecrated self, his highest self."

Nineteenth century British preacher Phillips Brooks defined preaching as "truth mediated through personality."

D. Martyn Lloyd-Jones said that in preaching "the whole personality of the preacher must be involved."

William Quayle wrote, "Preaching is the art of making a preacher and delivering that. The sermon is the man finding exposition for his soul."

Charles Jefferson said, "I prepare my sermons by preparing myself. Self-preparation is the most difficult work a preacher has to do."

In I Timothy 4:12, Paul told young Timothy not to allow anyone to look down on him or disparage him because of his age. Instead, he was to be an example. Set an example in speech, life, and character. It is not title, not rank, not degree that are here identified as necessary for credibility in effective ministry. Rather, what is required is a thorough testimony of godly living.

This intersects with the matter of fervency in preaching. By commending fervency or passion in the pulpit, I am not simply recommending high energy public speaking. We are not talking about volume. We are talking about sincere earnestness. There is a liberty in preaching that sincerity and a clean conscience generates.

I recall once hearing a pastor deliver a very colorful, dynamic message that seemed to captivate the crowd. A few weeks later I learned that this same man had been hiding a long-term immoral affair. He had finally been found out and was forced to resign from his church. I wondered, "How could such a man stand in front of a crowd and preach? How could he be so free and seemingly animated in the pulpit? Guilt must have tormented him as he spoke. His conscience must have restrained him." The explanation is actually very simple. How does any stage performer pretend to be what he is not? When a man speaks with a wounded conscience, he may still speak with fervency, but he ceases to be a preacher and becomes an actor. God help us to have a good conscience, and to "be sincere and without offence" (Phil. 1:10).

When a man speaks with a wounded conscience, he may still speak with fervency, but he ceases to be a preacher and becomes an actor.

I Timothy 4:15 tells us that this diligence is to be not only thorough but progressing. The preacher himself should be growing in grace (II Pet. 3:18). His spiritual progress needs to be evident to those who know him and watch him.

In Philippians 3, the apostle Paul confessed, "Not as though I had already attained either were already perfect..." He was saying that he had not arrived yet at the fullness of the perfection of Christ. He still had to progress. He still had to advance. If that was true of the great apostle, it is most certainly true of us. We cannot be complacent or satisfied with our spiritual attainments. We must let our "profiting appear to all."

In Acts 3, Peter told the lame man, "Such as I have give I thee." We should preach what we have first personally appropriated for ourselves from the word of

God. When our preaching reflects part of our own spiritual experience it will be fresh. We will have greater passion in our delivery. We preach it best when we feel it most.

Again, Charles Jefferson wrote, "If a man expects to move men by his preaching he must first do a deal of living, and the sooner he begins to live, the better."

Paul also says that in addition to ourselves, we must take heed to the doctrine or teaching. An effective preacher is a perpetual student. We must always be learning. And we must always be reviewing. D. Martyn Lloyd-Jones recommended the reading of theology for the preacher in order to maintain orthodoxy. We all have a fallen nature and a tendency to drift toward error.

But the order of these two considerations - take heed unto yourself and take heed to doctrine - is important. Take heed unto thyself comes first. This is not to suggest that doctrine is unimportant. It means, "be ye clean, that bear the vessels of the Lord" (Is. 52:11). It means, "The husbandman that laboreth must be first partaker of the fruits" (II Tim. 2:6). It means that hypocrisy is intolerable for the preacher.

Diligence in the business of the gospel ministry without diligence in my personal walk with God shows misplaced priorities.

Another aphorism penciled in my old Bible comes from the great missionary and translator, Henry Martyn: "Let me be reminded that the first great business in life is the sanctification of my own soul."

Diligence in the business of the gospel ministry without diligence in my personal walk with God shows misplaced priorities. Nothing is more important to the preacher (or any Christian) than his personal relationship with Christ.

II. Disciplined Consistency

Someone once said, "Consistency is the hallmark of the unimaginative." Emerson famously called "foolish consistency the hobgoblin of little minds." However, for the preacher there is nothing foolish about consistency. It is a great virtue. We need to grow, improve, and learn. But when it comes to taking heed to ourselves and the doctrine, we need to "continue in them." We need to be consistent. We need to be steady. We need to be constant.

The Lord told Joshua to be consistently in the word. "This book of the law shall not depart out of thy mouth; but thou shalt meditate therein day and night, that thou mayest observe to do according to all that is written therein: for then thou shalt make thy way prosperous, and then thou shalt have good success (Jos. 1:8).

Paul wrote to the Thessalonians to be consistently in prayer. "Pray without ceasing" (I Thes. 5:17).

The writer of Hebrews urged the saints to be consistently loving one another. "Let brotherly love continue" (Heb. 13:1).

When a man is consistent in his walk with God and in his labor in the word of God, the effect on his preaching will be notable.

Phillips Brooks, again in his Yale lectures, said this about fervency in preaching: "Nothing but fire kindles fire. To know in one's whole nature what it is to live by Christ; to be His; not our own; to be so occupied with gratitude for what He did for us and for what He continually is to us that His will and His glory shall be the sole aim of our life. I wish I could put in some words of new and overwhelming force that old accepted certainty that that is the first necessity of the preacher; that to preach without it is weary and unsatisfying and unprofitable work. That to preach with that is a perpetual privilege and joy."

William Quayle observed of Phillips Brooks himself, "Why did Phillips Brooks' preaching have such profound effect? some were asked. Voice, torrent of words, hugeness of physical size, wealth of ideas? Not these. 'The man; we felt him.' He drove through our veins like a bolt of fire. He was the sermon."

Dr. Bob Jones Jr. summarized all that we have said about fervency in preaching when he wrote: "The man who preaches with conviction of authority the words of divine authority backed up by a consistent life will always find a hearing."

FORMULA:
Conscience → Liberty → Fervency

Afterward

The following lines, written by Dr. Bob Jones Jr., have lingered in my mind since I first heard them recited decades ago. I often think of the last line as I approach the pulpit and pray, "Dear Lord, my people wait. Make this the shining hour."

Not every day the preacher's soul is fired.
But when the spark is there, foundations quake
And mountains move. Then sinful hearts,
inspired by judgment fears, to penitence awake.
Spirit anointed, most imperfect clay
Becomes a golden vessel for God's Word,
Which, overflowing, heals and cleans away
Black doubt and hind'ring fear.
Then Christians stirred
Know rushing mighty wind, baptizing fire,
Speaks such a preacher with a prophet's tone,
By love consumed, revival his desire,
Blessed beyond measure, pulpit then a throne.

Give to this preacher now the heavenly pow'r,
My people wait. Make this the shining hour.

Bibliography

Braga, James. *How to Prepare Bible Messages*. rev. ed. Portland, OR: Multnoma Press, 1981.

Broadus, John A. *On the Preparation and Delivery of Sermons*. 4th ed. San Francisco: Harper & Row, 1979.

Brooks, Phillips. *Lectures on Preaching*. London: H. R. Allenson LTD., nd.

Daane, James. *Preaching with Confidence*. Grand Rapids: Wm. B. Eerdmans Publishing Co., 1980.

Evans, William. *How to Prepare Sermons*. Chicago: Moody Press, 1964.

Hiebert, D. Edmond. *First Peter*. Chicago: Moody Press, 1984.

Jefferson, Charles E. *The Building of the Church*. New York: The MacMillen Company, 1910.

Jones, Bob. *How to Improve Your Preaching*. Greenville, SC: Bob Jones University Press, 1960.

Lloyd-Jones, David Martyn. *Preaching and Preachers*. Grand Rapids: Zondervan Publishing House, 1971.

McKechnie, Jean L. ed. *Webster's New Universal Unabridged Dictionary*. 2nd ed. New York: Simon & Schuster, 1983.

Parker, Joseph. *None Like It: A Plea for the Old Sword*. New York: Fleming H. Revell Company, 1893.

Perry, Lloyd M., and John R. Strubhar. *Evangelistic Preaching*. Chicago: Moody Press, 1979.

Quayle, William. *The Pastor-Preacher*. Cincinnati: Jennings & Graham, 1910.

Robinson, Haddon. *Biblical Preaching*. Grand Rapids: Baker Book House, 1980.

Spurgeon, Charles Haddon. *Lectures to My Students*. Grand Rapids: Baker Book House, 1977.

Wiersbe, Warren. *50 People Every Christian Should Know*. Grand Rapids: Baker Books, 2009.